Grade 1

Summer Skills
For the Child Going into First Grade

Written by **Christine Hood**

Illustrations by **Christine Schneider**

FlashKids

An imprint of Sterling Children's Books

Published by Sterling Publishing Co., Inc.
387 Park Avenue South, New York, NY 10016
Text and illustrations © 2005 by Flash Kids
Distributed in Canada by Sterling Publishing
c/o Canadian Manda Group, 165 Dufferin Street
Toronto, Ontario, Canada M6K 3H6
Distributed in the United Kingdom by GMC Distribution Services
Castle Place, 166 High Street, Lewes, East Sussex, England BN7 1XU
Distributed in Australia by Capricorn Link (Australia) Pty. Ltd.
P.O. Box 704, Windsor, NSW 2756, Australia

Sterling ISBN 978-1-4114-3410-3

Manufactured in Canada

Lot #:
2 4 6 8 10 9 7 5 3 1
03/10

For information about custom editions, special sales, premium and
corporate purchases, please contact Sterling Special Sales
Department at 800-805-5489 or specialsales@sterlingpublishing.com.

Cover design and production by Mada Design, Inc.

DEAR PARENT,

Your child is out of school for the summer, but this doesn't mean that learning has to stop! In fact, reinforcing academic skills in the summer months will help your child succeed during the next school year. This Summer Skills workbook provides activities to keep your child engaged in all the subject areas—Language Arts, Math, Social Studies, and Science—during the summer months. The activities increase in difficulty as the book progresses by reviewing what your child learned in kindergarten and then introducing skills for first grade. This will help build your child's confidence and help him or her get excited for the new school year!

As you and your child go through the book, look for "Fast Fact" or "On Your Own" features that build upon the theme or activity on each page. At the back of this book you'll find a comprehensive reading list. Keep your child interested in reading by providing some or all of the books on the list for your child to read. You will also find a list of suggested summer projects at the back of this book. These are fun activities for you and your child to complete together. Use all of these special features to continue exploring and learning about different concepts all summer long!

As your child completes the activities in this book, shower him or her with encouragement and praise. You can feel good knowing that you are taking an active and important role in your child's education. Helping your child complete the activities in this book provides him or her with an excellent example—that you value learning, every day! Have a wonderful summer, and most of all, have fun learning together!

TABLE OF CONTENTS

ALL ABOUT ME!

Ask a parent to help you write about yourself on the lines below.
Then tape a photo or draw a picture of yourself in the box.

My name is _____.

I am _____ years old.

I was born on _____.

I have _____ hair.

I have _____ eyes.

My mother's name is _____.

My father's name is _____.

My favorite food is _____.

My favorite color is _____.

My favorite book is _____.

My favorite movie is _____.

My favorite things to do are _____

_____

_____.

My brothers and sisters are

_____.

_____.

_____.

Me

ON YOUR OWN
Have a parent help you make a family book! Copy this page and fill it in for each family member. This would make a great gift!

BALLOON MATCH

Match each numeral to its number word.
Then color the balloon pairs the same color.

ON YOUR OWN
How high can you count? Write down the
numbers as you count aloud. Then see
how many number words you can write!

ALPHABET ACTION

Fill in the missing letters of the alphabet.

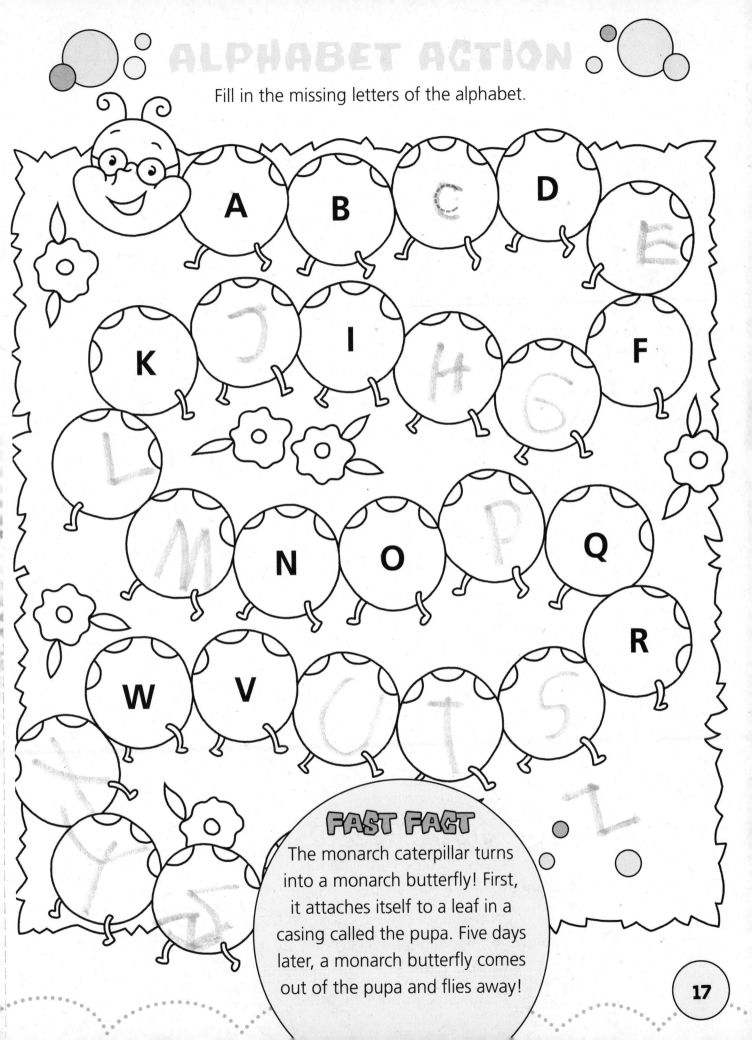

FAST FACT

The monarch caterpillar turns into a monarch butterfly! First, it attaches itself to a leaf in a casing called the pupa. Five days later, a monarch butterfly comes out of the pupa and flies away!

17

ANIMAL ALPHABET

Write the names of these animals in alphabetical order.

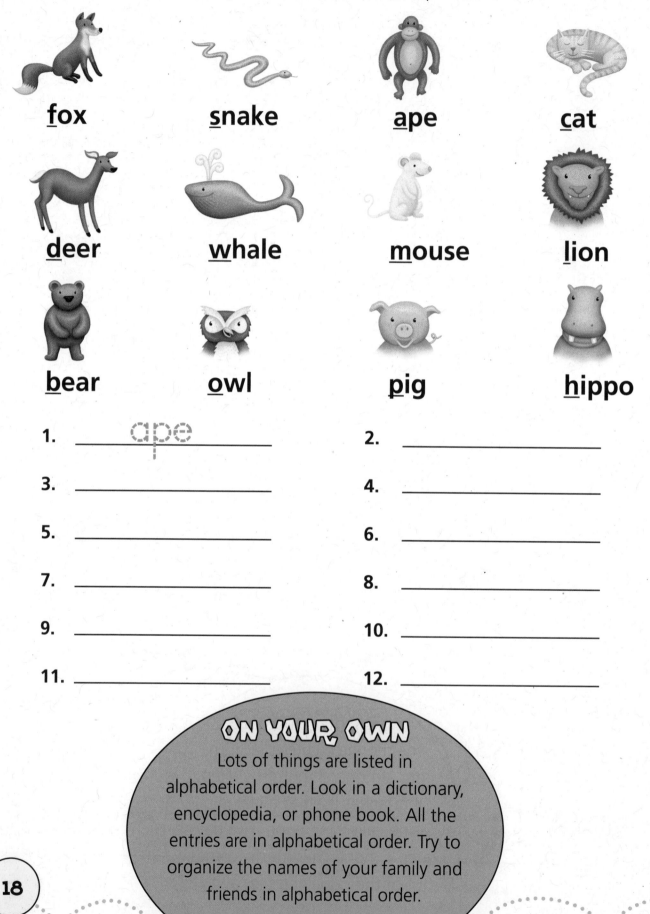

fox   snake   ape   cat

deer   whale   mouse   lion

bear   owl   pig   hippo

1. ___ape___

2. _____

3. _____

4. _____

5. _____

6. _____

7. _____

8. _____

9. _____

10. _____

11. _____

12. _____

ON YOUR OWN

Lots of things are listed in alphabetical order. Look in a dictionary, encyclopedia, or phone book. All the entries are in alphabetical order. Try to organize the names of your family and friends in alphabetical order.

18

CARING AND SHARING

It's important to be nice to others. Color the pictures that show children caring for and sharing with each other.

ON YOUR OWN

Families work together. How do you help your family at home? Do you set the table? Do you feed the pets? Do you clean your room? Think up more ways you can help at home.

SHAPES, SHAPES, SHAPES!

Look at each picture below. What shape do you see?
Write the shape word under each picture.

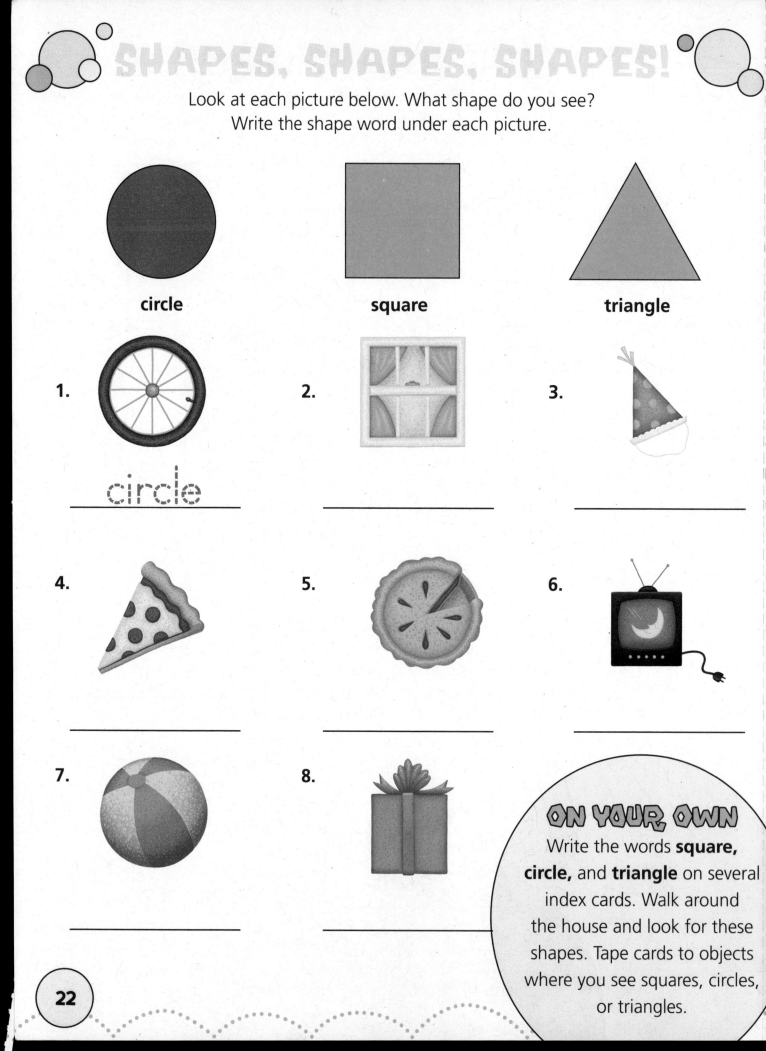

circle

square

triangle

1.

circle

2.

3.

4.

5.

6.

7.

8.

ON YOUR OWN

Write the words **square, circle,** and **triangle** on several index cards. Walk around the house and look for these shapes. Tape cards to objects where you see squares, circles, or triangles.

HOORAY FOR LONG A!

The **a** sound you hear in the word **cake** is the **long a** sound.
Say the name of each object. Color the objects that have the **long a** sound.

bug

grapes

cup

ape

broom

cow

goat

plane

dog

snake

sail

ON YOUR OWN
How many foods can you name that begin with the letter **a**? Make a list!

gate

SEE THE LONG E!

The **e** sound you hear in the word **feet** is the **long e** sound.
Say the name of each object. Color the objects that have the **long e** sound.

kite

hen

seal

bee

clock

milk

bed

sheep

peas

tree

leaf

book

Trace the words for each American symbol.

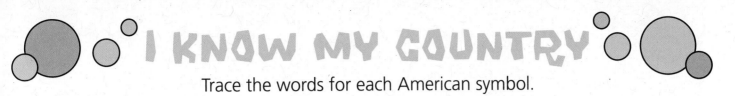

This is the American flag.

It has 50 stars and 13 stripes.

This is a bald eagle.

It is the American national bird.

This is the Statue of Liberty.

It is a symbol of freedom.

Write one thing you know about one of these American symbols.

_____

- -

_____

- -

_____

- -

_____

CHANGE CHALLENGE

Circle the coins to match the amount shown.

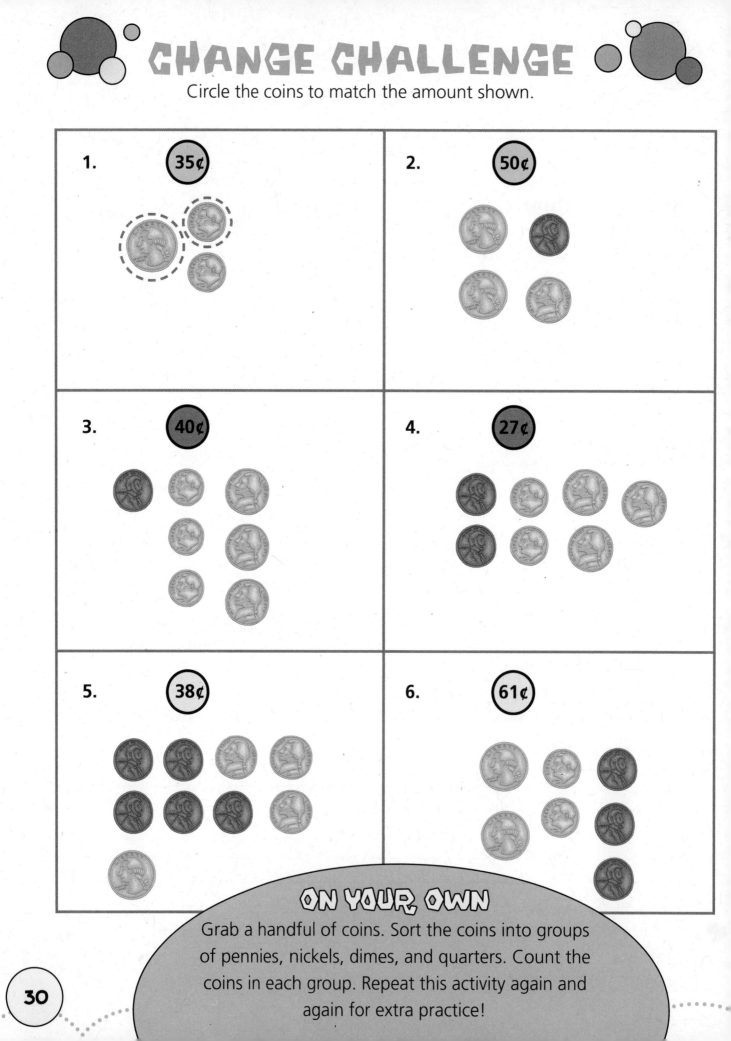

1. 35¢

2. 50¢

3. 40¢

4. 27¢

5. 38¢

6. 61¢

ON YOUR OWN

Grab a handful of coins. Sort the coins into groups of pennies, nickels, dimes, and quarters. Count the coins in each group. Repeat this activity again and again for extra practice!

Circle the heavier object in each box.

Circle the lighter object in each box.

ON YOUR OWN

Weigh yourself on a scale.
Write down your weight. Then walk
around your house and look for things
that weigh more or less than you do.
Make a list of the things you find.

MEASURING MICE

Use a ruler to measure each mouse.

1. _2 inches_

2. _____

3. _____

4. _____

5. _____

6. _____

LETTER MIX-UP

Below are the mixed-up letters of a word. How many little words can you make from the letters? Can you find the BIG word?

a   n   t   i   r

Words with 2 letters:

_____

_____

_____

_____

Word with 4 letters:

_____

Words with 3 letters:

_____

_____

_____

_____

_____

_____

ON YOUR OWN

Write the name of your favorite animal. See how many words you can make from the letters in the animal's name.

The BIG word: _____

Draw a picture of the BIG word below. Here's a hint: It is a fun way to travel.

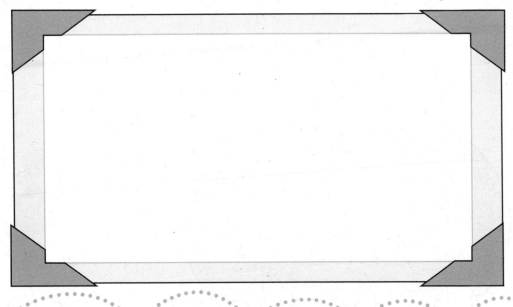

DAY AT THE BEACH

Look at the summer words in the word box.
Find and circle the words in the word search.
They can go across or down.

sun	shell	fish	sand
waves	sea	pail	crab

F I I S H R W

J A U S E A

I S N H D V

N C O E B E

A R W L O S

P A I L R E

O B S A N D

ON YOUR OWN

Write about or draw a picture of
a day you spent at the beach. If
you have not been to the beach,
write or draw about what you
would like to see there.

34

The **i** sound you hear in the word **smile** is the **long i** sound.
Say the name of each object. Color the objects that have the **long i** sound.

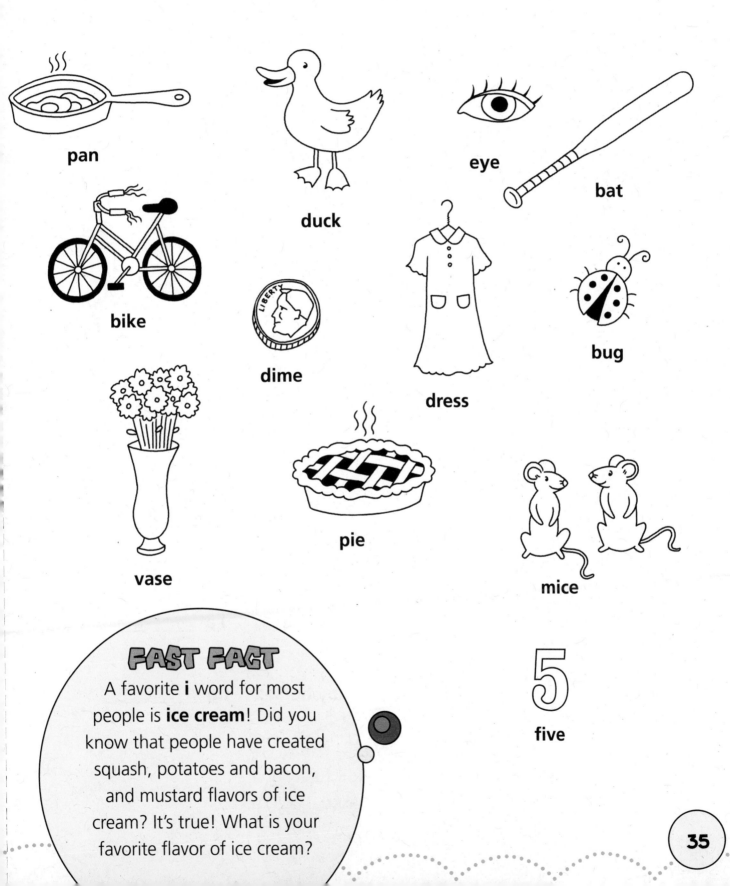

pan

duck

eye

bat

bike

dime

dress

bug

vase

pie

mice

FAST FACT

A favorite **i** word for most people is **ice cream**! Did you know that people have created squash, potatoes and bacon, and mustard flavors of ice cream? It's true! What is your favorite flavor of ice cream?

5

five

MOTHERS AND BABIES

Draw a line to match each mother animal to her baby.

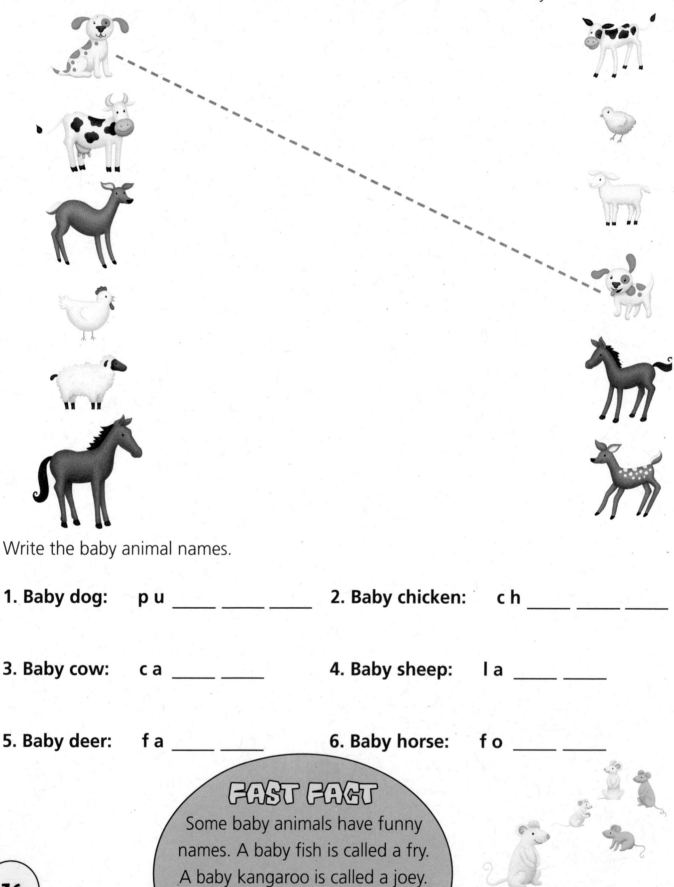

Write the baby animal names.

1. Baby dog: p u ____ ____ ____

2. Baby chicken: c h ____ ____ ____

3. Baby cow: c a ____ ____

4. Baby sheep: l a ____ ____

5. Baby deer: f a ____ ____

6. Baby horse: f o ____ ____

FAST FACT

Some baby animals have funny names. A baby fish is called a fry. A baby kangaroo is called a joey. A baby mouse is called a pinkie.

ON THE MAP

Use the words in the word box to fill in the names of the things you see on the map.

park	school	road	river
mountain	hospital	lake	library

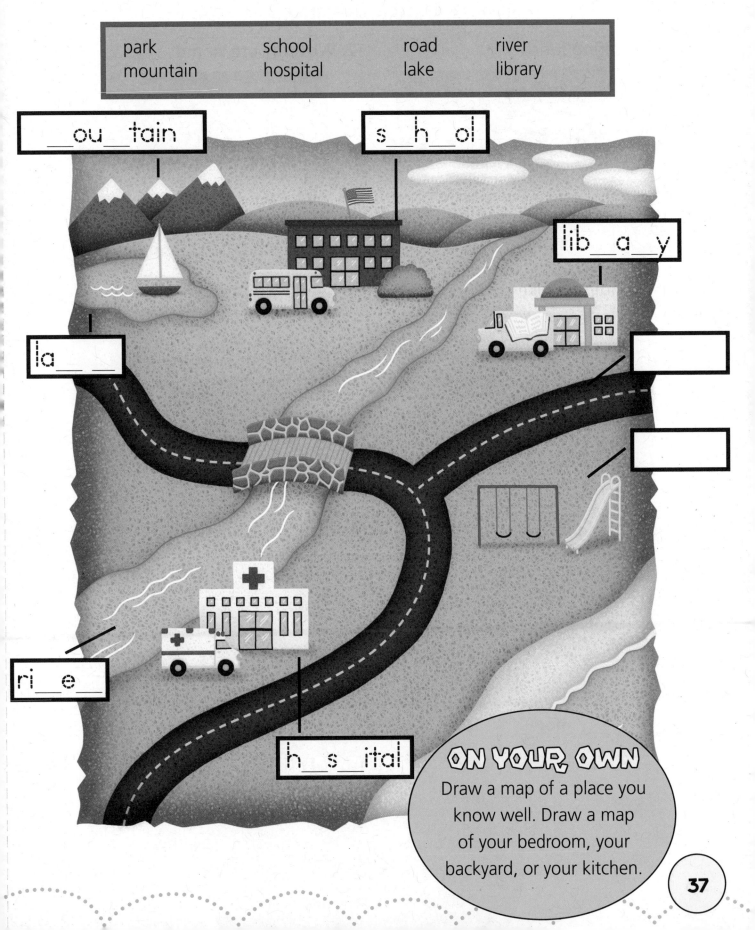

__ou__tain

s__h__ol

lib__a__y

la____

ri__e__

h__s__ital

ON YOUR OWN

Draw a map of a place you know well. Draw a map of your bedroom, your backyard, or your kitchen.

IN A MINUTE

Look at each picture. Does each activity take more or less than one minute? Circle **more** or **less**.

1. Eating lunch

(more)   less

2. Writing your name

more   less

3. Riding a bike to school

more   less

4. Reading a book

more   less

5. Doing a somersault

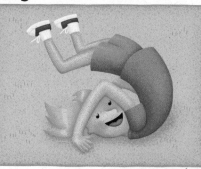

more   less

6. Kicking a ball

more   less

ON YOUR OWN

What can you do in a minute? Can you brush your teeth? Tie your shoes? Have a parent use a kitchen timer to time various activities.

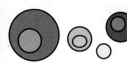

SUNDAY IS A FUN DAY

Trace the name of each day of the week.

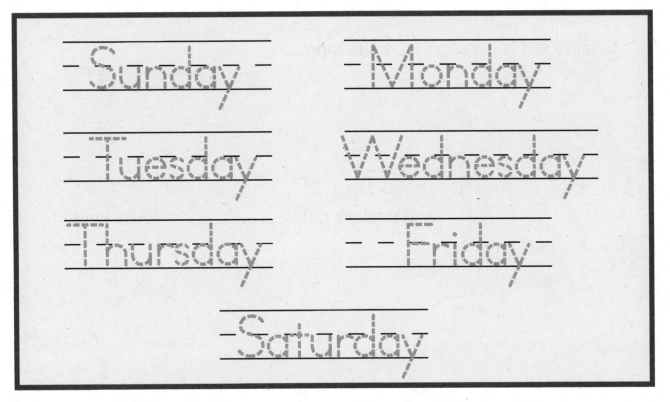

Sunday   Monday

Tuesday   Wednesday

Thursday   Friday

Saturday

What is your favorite day of the week? Write the name of the day. Then draw a picture of something you like to do on that day.

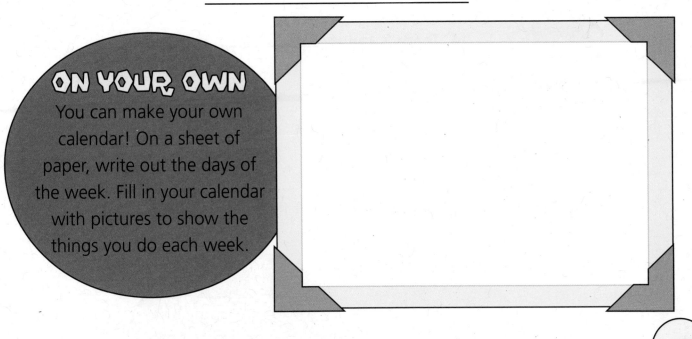

ON YOUR OWN

You can make your own calendar! On a sheet of paper, write out the days of the week. Fill in your calendar with pictures to show the things you do each week.

CAT TAILS

How long is each cat's tail? Count the units.

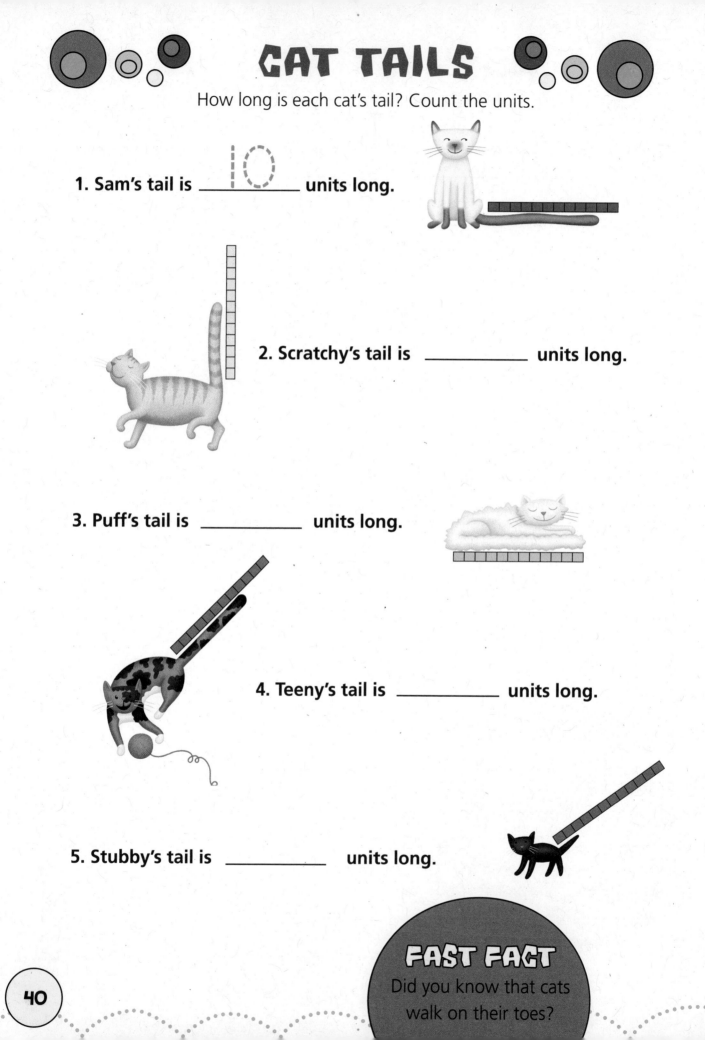

1. Sam's tail is __10__ units long.

2. Scratchy's tail is _____ units long.

3. Puff's tail is _____ units long.

4. Teeny's tail is _____ units long.

5. Stubby's tail is _____ units long.

FAST FACT
Did you know that cats walk on their toes?

ALWAYS OPPOSITE

Jack Rabbit always changes his mind. Draw a line matching the opposites below.

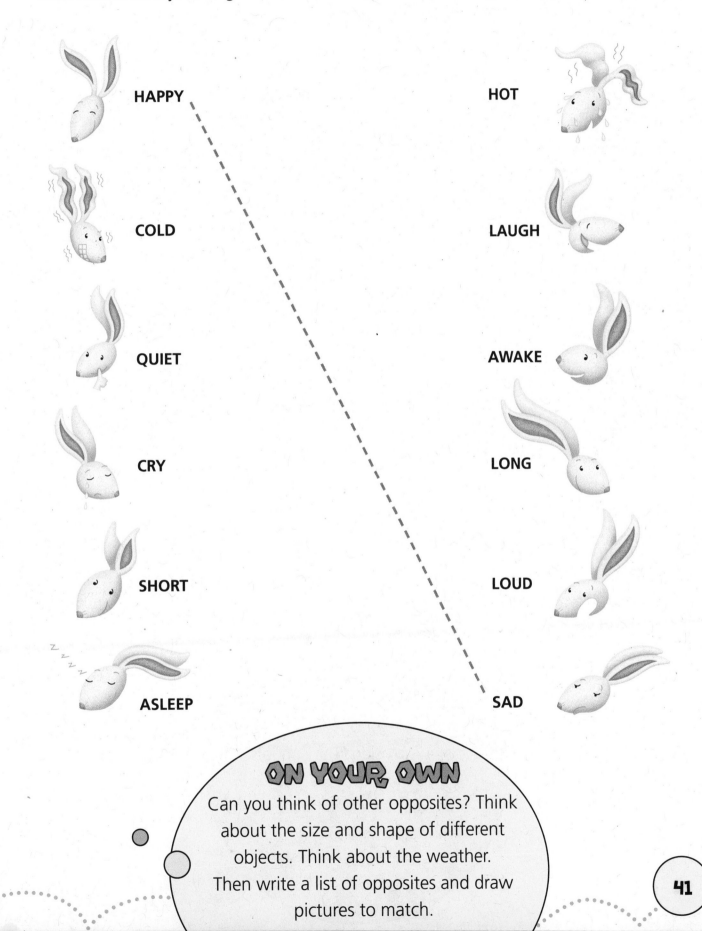

HAPPY

COLD

QUIET

CRY

SHORT

ASLEEP

HOT

LAUGH

AWAKE

LONG

LOUD

SAD

ON YOUR OWN

Can you think of other opposites? Think about the size and shape of different objects. Think about the weather. Then write a list of opposites and draw pictures to match.

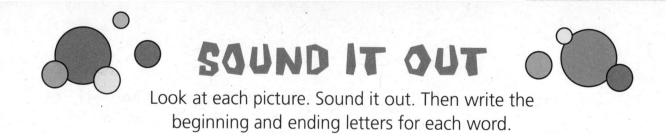

SOUND IT OUT

Look at each picture. Sound it out. Then write the
beginning and ending letters for each word.

1. c o a t

2. R e a D

3. B o a t

4. S e a l

5. __ o a __

6. __ e a __

7. __ o a __

8. M e a t

HELLO, LONG O!

The **o** sound you hear in the word **rose** is the **long o** sound.
Say the name of each object. Color the objects that have the **long o** sound.

soap

snake

sheep

rope

hoe

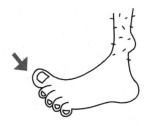

toe

light

fox

car

bird

bow

ON YOUR OWN

Choose a word that begins with the letter **o**, like **octopus** or **oatmeal**. Write the letters down the side of a piece of paper. Using each letter to begin a word or phrase, write something that describes the **o** word.

43

THE FOUR SEASONS

There are four seasons. They are called **winter, spring, summer,** and **fall**.
Look at each object. Which season does it remind you of?
Write **winter, spring, summer,** or **fall**.

1. ___winter___

2. _____

3. _____

4. _____

5. _____

6. _____

7. _____

8. _____

9. _____

10. _____

ON YOUR OWN

What is your favorite season? Do you like to swim in the summer?
Do you like to build snowmen in the winter? Write a few words or sentences
about why you like this season. Then draw a picture to go with what you wrote.

WHERE DOES IT COME FROM?

Can you tell where things come from? Draw a line to match the three pictures that go together.

FAST FACT

Did you know that chocolate comes from a bean? It is called the cocoa bean. Cocoa beans come from the fruit on cacao trees. These trees grow in warm places like Africa and Central and South America.

WHAT TIME IS IT?

Draw the minute hand and the hour hand on each clock to show the time.

minute hand ———→

hour hand ———→

It's 9:30.

1.  7:30

2.  12:00

3.  9:00

4.  11:30

5.  6:00

6.  2:30

7.  5:30

8.  4:00

9.  10:00

FAST FACT
The most expensive watch in the world was sold in 1999. It cost 11 million dollars!

PRETTY PATTERNS

Find the shirts with matching patterns. Color each pair alike.

ON YOUR OWN

Look at the clothes in your closet. What patterns do you see there? Draw pictures of some of the patterns you see.

47

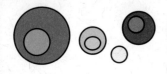

WHO IS SWIMMING?

Connect the dots from **1** to **30**. Then color the picture.

FAST FACT

Dolphins are mammals, not fish. Dolphins are very playful animals that love to jump. Some dolphins can jump 16 feet in the air!

LONG U, TOO!

The **u** sound you hear in the word **blue** is the **long u** sound.
Say the name of each object. Color the objects that have the **long u** sound.

mule

fish

apple

unicorn

boat

spoon

horse

cap

broom

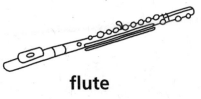

flute

cube

FAST FACT
Unicorns are mythical creatures from ancient times. Some people thought the unicorn's horn was protection against poison. What do you think? Do you think unicorns are real?

glue

LISTEN FOR SOUNDS

Say each word aloud. Then draw a line from each object on the left to an object on the right with the same short-vowel sound.

a as in **apple**   **e** as in **end**   **i** as in **inch**

o as in **ox**   **u** as in **up**

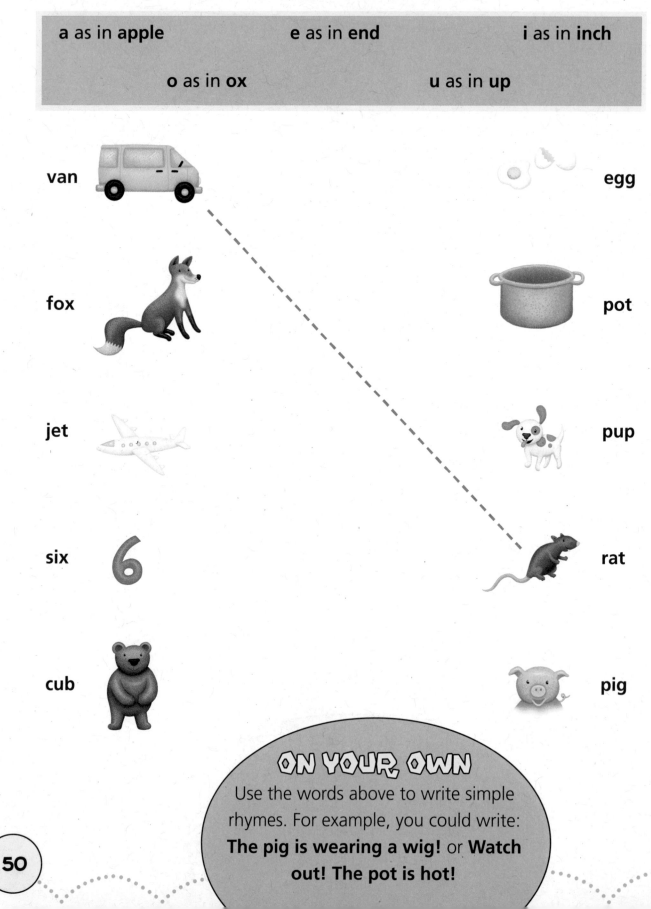

van

fox

jet

six

cub

egg

pot

pup

rat

pig

ON YOUR OWN

Use the words above to write simple rhymes. For example, you could write: **The pig is wearing a wig!** or **Watch out! The pot is hot!**

READY TO RHYME

Say the name for each picture.
Then circle the words in each row that rhyme with the picture word.

1. lid   (tune)   (noon)   bell

2. lake   rock   steak   box

3. boat   sand   bee   sea

4. sock   kite   jump   rock

5. snow   meet   ring   swing

6. well   rain   good   plane

ON YOUR OWN
Think up at least two more rhyming words for each picture.

MY FIVE SENSES

Write the name of the sense under the picture.

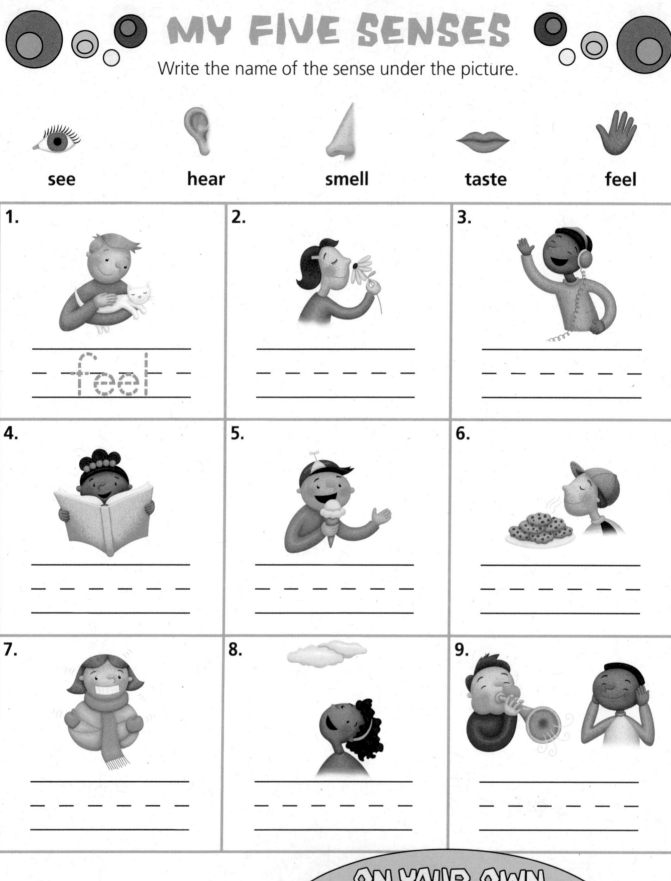

see   hear   smell   taste   feel

1. feel

2. _____

3. _____

4. _____

5. _____

6. _____

7. _____

8. _____

9. _____

ON YOUR OWN

Go somewhere with lots of sights and sounds. Try a park, zoo, or restaurant. Describe to a friend everything you hear, see, smell, feel, and taste.

MY COMMUNITY

Many people help us in our community.
Write the word that tells about each helper. Use the words in the box.

sick	pet	fires	read	teeth	safe

1. A doctor helps me when I am _____ sick _____.

2. A teacher helps me learn how to ___ r _____.

3. A firefighter puts out ___ f _____.

4. A vet helps me care for my ___ p _____.

5. A dentist helps me have healthy ___ t _____.

6. A police officer keeps the community ___ s _____.

Draw a picture of your favorite community helper.

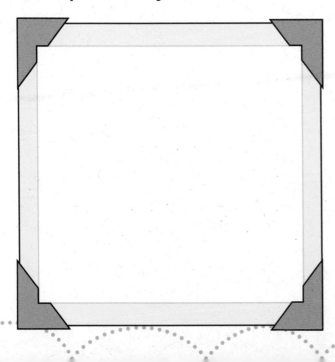

FAST FACT

Some veterinarians work only with zoo animals. They work with the smallest insect to the largest elephant. Can you imagine what it would be like to give an elephant medicine?

CROSS IT OUT

Follow the directions to find the answers.

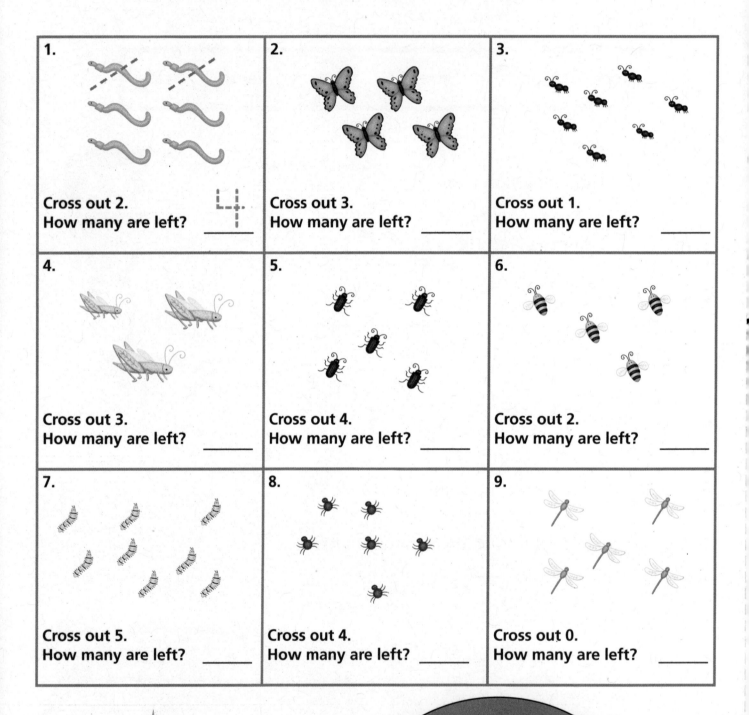

1.

Cross out 2.
How many are left? 4

2.

Cross out 3.
How many are left? _____

3.

Cross out 1.
How many are left? _____

4.

Cross out 3.
How many are left? _____

5.

Cross out 4.
How many are left? _____

6.

Cross out 2.
How many are left? _____

7.

Cross out 5.
How many are left? _____

8.

Cross out 4.
How many are left? _____

9.

Cross out 0.
How many are left? _____

FAST FACT

Spiders are not insects. They are called arachnids. Most scientists believe the most poisonous spider in the world is the black widow.

SHAPE GARDEN

Color the shapes. Use the Color Key to find out which colors to use.

Color Key

blue   green   yellow   pink

purple   orange   red

ON YOUR OWN

Cut out several circles, squares, triangles, and hearts from construction paper. Have a parent cut each shape in half using a jagged line, like a puzzle piece. See if you can match up all the shapes!

FARM FRIENDS

Color the animals in each row that are alike.

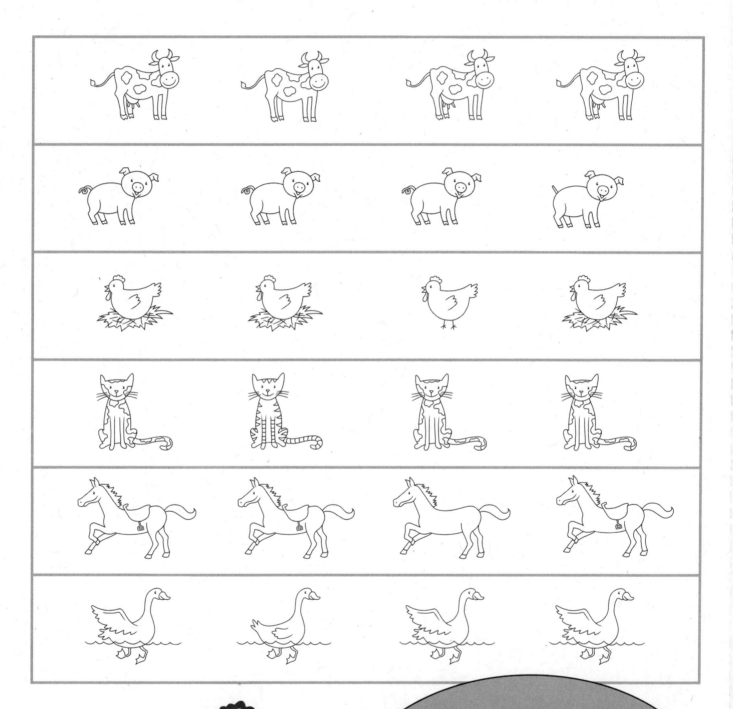

ON YOUR OWN

Visit a nearby farm or petting zoo. If you are able to pet the animals, notice how they're different from pets you have at home. For example, sheep have puffy wool coats and pigs have bristled hair.

LISTEN UP!

Look at the objects in each group.
Say the names of each aloud.
Then circle the short-vowel sound you hear in each group.

1.
a e i o u

2.
a e i o u

3.
a e i o u

4.
a e i o u

5.
a e i o u

6.
a e i o u

7.
a e i o u

8.
a e i o u

9.
a e i o u

ON YOUR OWN

On index cards, write these and other short-vowel words. Mix up the cards, then group each card according to the vowel sound you hear: **a, e, i, o,** or **u**.

BUSY, BUZZY BEE

Help Buzzy Bee find her friends.
Draw a line to connect letters that spell out a sentence. Write the sentence below.

_____

- - - - - - - - - - - - - - - -

_____

- - - - - - - - - - - - - - - -

_____

KINDS OF SENTENCES

A **statement** tells something. It ends with a period. (**.**)
A **question** asks something. It ends with a question mark. (**?**)

Read each sentence aloud or have a parent read it to you. Then tell if it is a **statement** or a **question**. Circle **S** or **Q**.

1. **The kite is in the tree.**   S   Q

2. **Mia loves to dance.**   S   Q

3. **Did Josh eat the cookies?**   S   Q

4. **The ants are on the hill.**   S   Q

5. **Where are we going for lunch?**   S   Q

6. **Is the mouse under the bed?**   S   Q

7. **Jack played with his dog.**   S   Q

8. **I picked a daisy in the garden.**   S   Q

9. **Do you like ice cream?**   S   Q

10. **The long snake is red and black.**   S   Q

ON YOUR OWN
Having good manners helps us get along with other people. With a parent or friend, act out scenes in which you are asking questions and saying polite and caring things. For example: "May I please borrow your crayons?" "Thank you for the gift." "I'm sorry I broke the cup." "I love you."

WHAT WILL I WEAR?

Circle the things you would wear in each kind of weather.

It is snowing.	
It is sunny.	
It is raining.	

FAST FACT
People wear extra clothes to keep warm in the winter. Since animals don't wear clothes, they keep warm by growing thicker fur!

STAYING SAFE

Look at each picture. Some children are being safe.
Some children are not being safe. Color the pictures that show children being safe.
Cross out the pictures that show children being unsafe.

ON YOUR OWN

Take a walk with a parent. Talk about how to be safe on
your street and in your neighborhood. Read and discuss the
meanings of traffic signs. Talk about how to ride a bike safely
and about neighbors you can count on.

61

JUNGLE FUN

Color **red** in the areas that add up to the numbers **0, 1,** or **2**.
Color **green** in the areas that add up to the numbers **3, 4,** or **5**.
Color **brown** in the areas that add up to the numbers **6, 7,** or **8**.
Color yellow in the areas that add up to the numbers 9 or 10.

FAST FACT

One of the most famous monkeys in the world was Ham the chimp. In 1961, Ham was the first chimp to go into space. This amazing monkey learned how to press levers and buttons for the mission. He was rewarded with banana pellets!

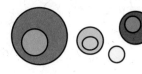 # SEEING SPOTS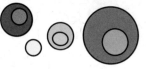

Count the spots on each ladybug.
Then add the numbers.

1.   +   =   9

2.   +   =

3.   +   =

4.   +   =

5.   +   =

6.   +   =

7.   +   =

8.   +   =

FAST FACT
Ladybugs make a chemical that smells and tastes bad. They shoot out this chemical from their legs to keep birds from eating them!

PATTERN PATHS

Look at the numbers in each row. Then finish the pattern.

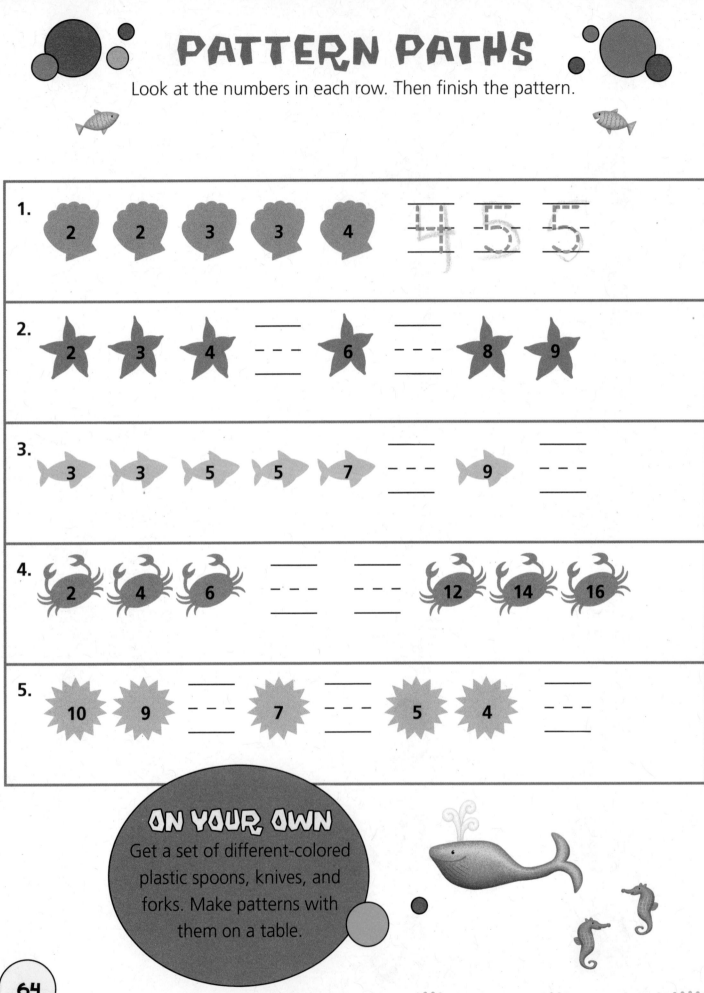

1. 2 2 3 3 4 4 5 5

2. 2 3 4 ___ 6 ___ 8 9

3. 3 3 5 5 7 ___ 9 ___

4. 2 4 6 ___ ___ 12 14 16

5. 10 9 ___ 7 ___ 5 4 ___

ON YOUR OWN
Get a set of different-colored plastic spoons, knives, and forks. Make patterns with them on a table.

DRAW THE WORD

Describing words give details about an object.
Draw an object for each word below.

Draw something **furry**.

Draw something **tasty**.

Draw something **sticky**.

Draw something **funny**.

ON YOUR OWN
Look around your house and in your yard for other things that are **furry, tasty, sticky,** and **funny**. Draw pictures of the things you find.

WORD GROUPS

Write each word in the correct circle.

bread	blue	red	square	milk
circle	grapes	star	green	pizza
triangle	brown	beans	oval	yellow

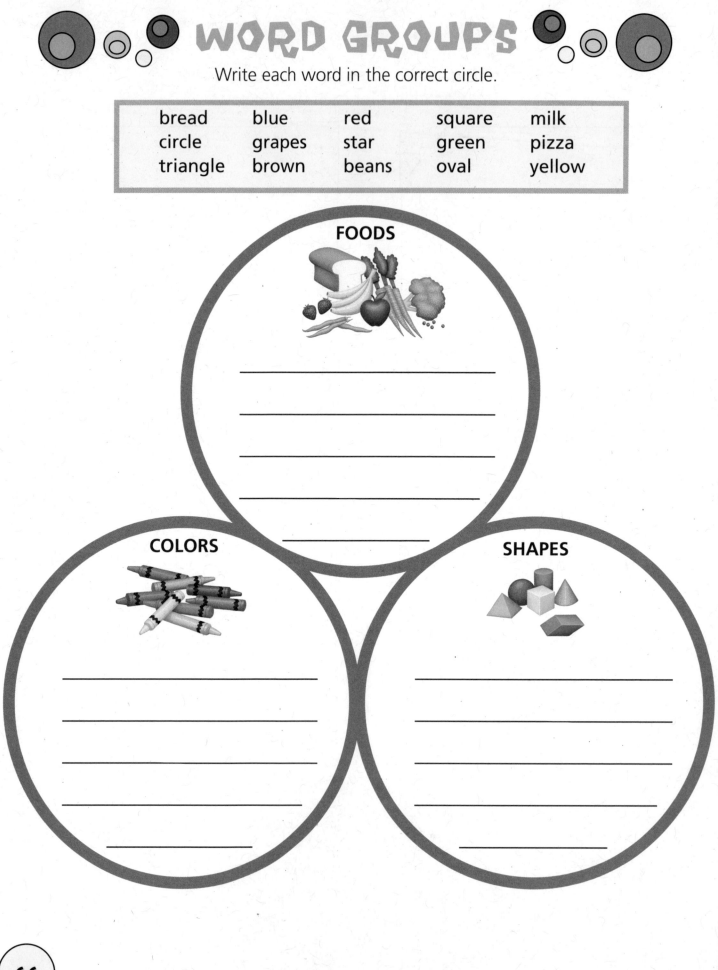

FOODS

_____

_____

_____

_____

COLORS

_____

_____

_____

_____

SHAPES

_____

_____

_____

_____

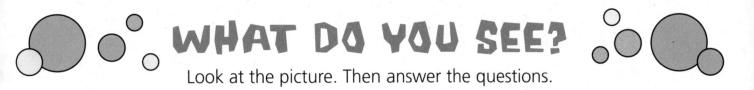

WHAT DO YOU SEE?

Look at the picture. Then answer the questions.

Circle your answer.

1. Where is this scene?	beach	zoo	(park)
2. Who is on the swing?	dog	girl	boy
3. What is in the tree?	cat	bear	bird
4. Who is on the slide?	girl	woman	boy
5. A woman is walking her:	pig	dog	cat
6. The woman's shirt is:	white	red	blue

ON YOUR OWN

Go somewhere with a parent where there are a lot of people. Talk about all the details you see. Do you see animals? What colors are people wearing? Do you hear music, feel wind, or smell the ocean?

67

BEARS, BIRDS, AND BEES

Color the animals. Then trace the animal names below.

bee

bear

bird

FAST FACT
There are eight kinds of bears in the world. There are brown bears, Malayan Sun bears, Polar bears, Asiatic black bears, American black bears, giant pandas, sloth bears, and spectacled bears. That's a lot of bears!

THEN AND NOW

Long ago, people used different objects to live and travel than we use today.
Use **blue** to color the objects from long ago.
Use yellow to color the objects from today.

1. How do we travel?

2. How do we keep in touch with others?

3. What do we use every day?

    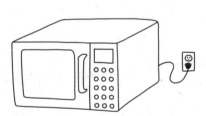

COUNTING COINS

Count the coins in each row. Write the total value of each group of coins.

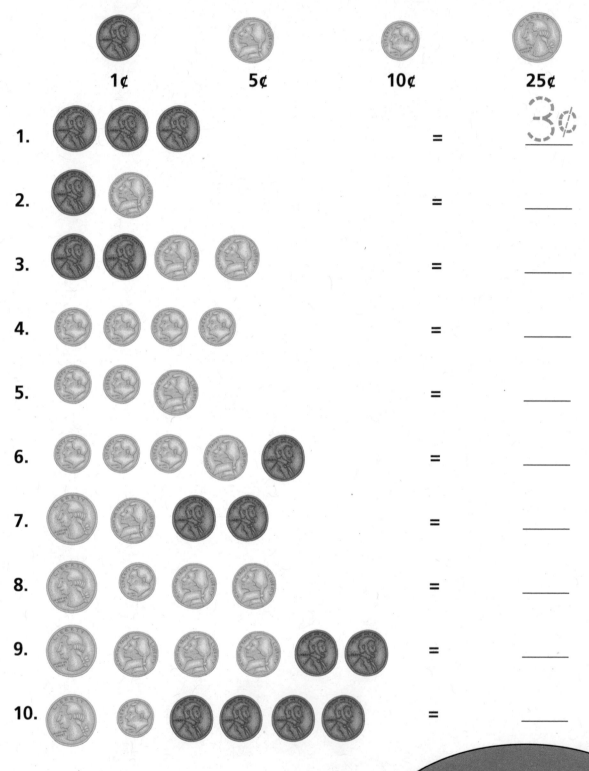

	1¢	5¢	10¢	25¢

1. = 3¢

2. = ____

3. = ____

4. = ____

5. = ____

6. = ____

7. = ____

8. = ____

9. = ____

10. = ____

ON YOUR OWN
What can you buy with one dollar?
With a parent, go to the market
and find all the things you can buy
for one dollar or less.

COLOR QUIZ

Follow the directions to find the answers.

1.

Color 4.
How many are left? _____

2.

Color 1.
How many are left? _____

3.

Color 3.
How many are left? _____

4.

Color 2.
How many are left? _____

5.

Color 1.
How many are left? _____

6.

Color 6.
How many are left? _____

7.

Color 5.
How many are left? _____

8.

Color 5.
How many are left? _____

9.

Color 2.
How many are left? _____

ON YOUR OWN

On a sunny day, have a parent use a garden hose to spray a mist of water across the Sun's rays. Stand with your back to the Sun and look for a rainbow in the mist. Can you name all the colors in the rainbow?

ALL DAY LONG

Look at each picture. Read the sentence.
Circle **morning** or **night** to show when you do each activity.

1. He's going to school.

(morning)   night

2. She's going to bed.

morning   night

3. She's eating breakfast.

morning   night

4. He's brushing his teeth.

morning   night

5. He's eating dinner.

morning   night

6. She's getting dressed.

morning   night

ON YOUR OWN

Find all the timepieces in your house. Look for a kitchen clock, clock radio, watches, timers, and more. With a parent, talk about how all these different timepieces keep and show time.

BUILD A SANDWICH

Write the numbers **1** to **6** to put the steps in order.

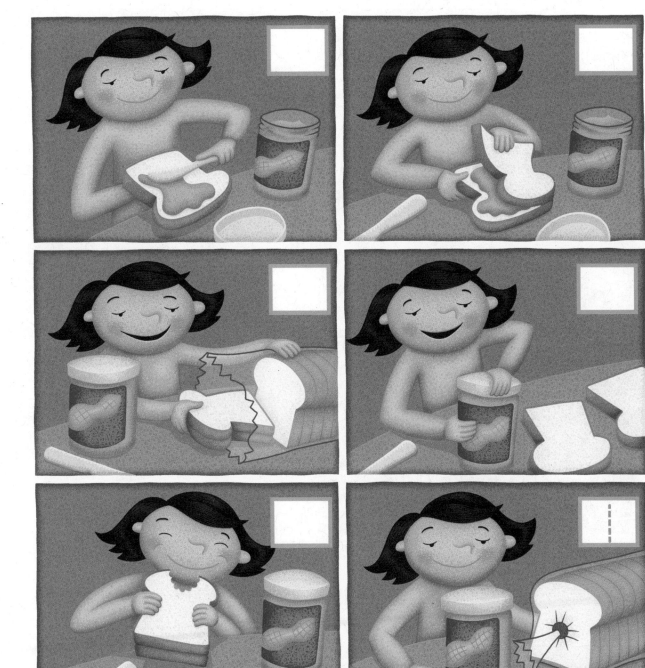

ON YOUR OWN

Think of something simple you can do, like make toast or ride a bike. Write the directions with pictures or words. Try to include at least three steps.

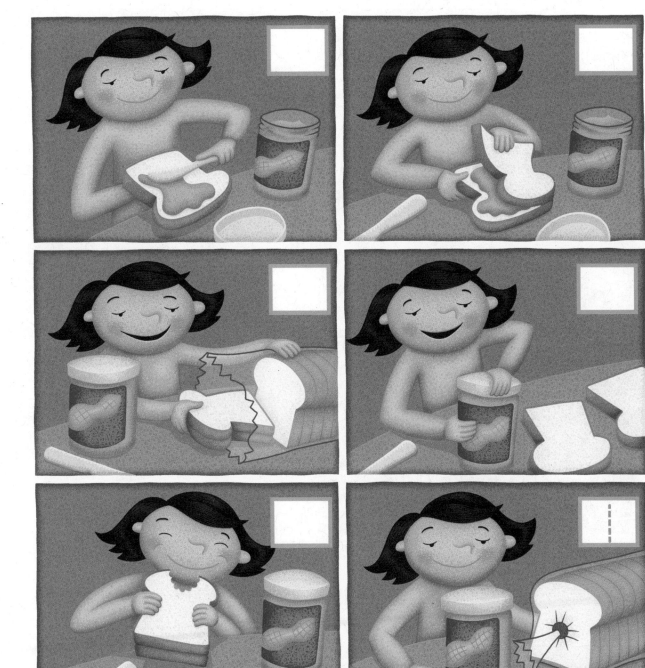

PHOTO CLUES

Look at the photo. Then finish the story using the words in the box.

monkey	peanuts	zoo	elephant
zebras	snakes	dad	lion

ZEBRAS

SNAKES

My family went to the ____ZOO____. We had so much fun! First, my

_____ got me a toy _____ at the gift shop. We fed a big gray

_____. We fed him lots of _____. Then I saw a funny

_____ in a tree! We saw more animals too. The sign told us where to

find _____ and _____. I liked the elephant the best. I love

the zoo!

74

With a parent, read the story. Then answer the questions.

One very hot day, Fox was walking in a field. He was very thirsty. He saw some grapes hanging from a vine. The grapes looked plump and juicy. Fox licked his dry lips. The grapes looked delicious! Fox decided he must have some grapes. He jumped high. But he could not reach the juicy fruit. Fox jumped over and over again. But the grapes were just out of reach. Finally, Fox sat down in the dirt. He was very thirsty. He was too tired to jump anymore. He said, "Those grapes are probably sour anyway!" Fox put his nose in the air and walked away.

Say or write the answers to these questions.

1. Who is the character in this story? _____

2. Where does this story take place? _____

3. How did the story start? _____

4. How did the story end? _____

5. What was the character's problem? _____

FAST FACT
This story is called a fable. A fable usually teaches a lesson. The lesson learned from this fable is: "It is easy to dislike what you can not have."

PEANUT BUTTER SCIENCE

With a parent, make this fun-to-eat play dough!

Recipe

You will need:

$\frac{3}{4}$ cup peanut butter

$\frac{3}{4}$ cup toasted wheat germ

$\frac{1}{2}$ cup honey

$\frac{1}{4}$ cup powdered milk

Mix all ingredients until smooth. Store in an airtight container.

Talk about these questions with a parent.

1. Look at each item as you put it in the bowl.
- How does it feel?
- How does it smell?
- Is it a liquid or a solid?

2. Describe the dough.
- Is it soft or hard?
- Is it wet or dry?

3. Shape the dough with your hands.
- Stretch it. Squeeze it.
- Shape it into an object.

Draw a picture of your object. You can even eat it! Yum!

FAST FACT

Dr. George Washington Carver is known as the "father of the peanut." He developed over 300 uses for this special nut!

I ♥ THE EARTH!

Learn what you can do to help the Earth! Color the pictures. Write one way you can love the Earth on page **7** of your cut-out book below. Draw a picture too! Cut out the pages below. Put the pages in order, then staple them together on the left side. Read your book with a parent!

I ♥ the earth.
1

I can water flowers.
3

I can plant trees.
5

I can _____.
7

FAST FACT
The Earth is about four and a half billion years old!

I ♥ THE EARTH!

Color the pictures. Write one way you can love the Earth on page **8** of your cut-out book below. Draw a picture too!

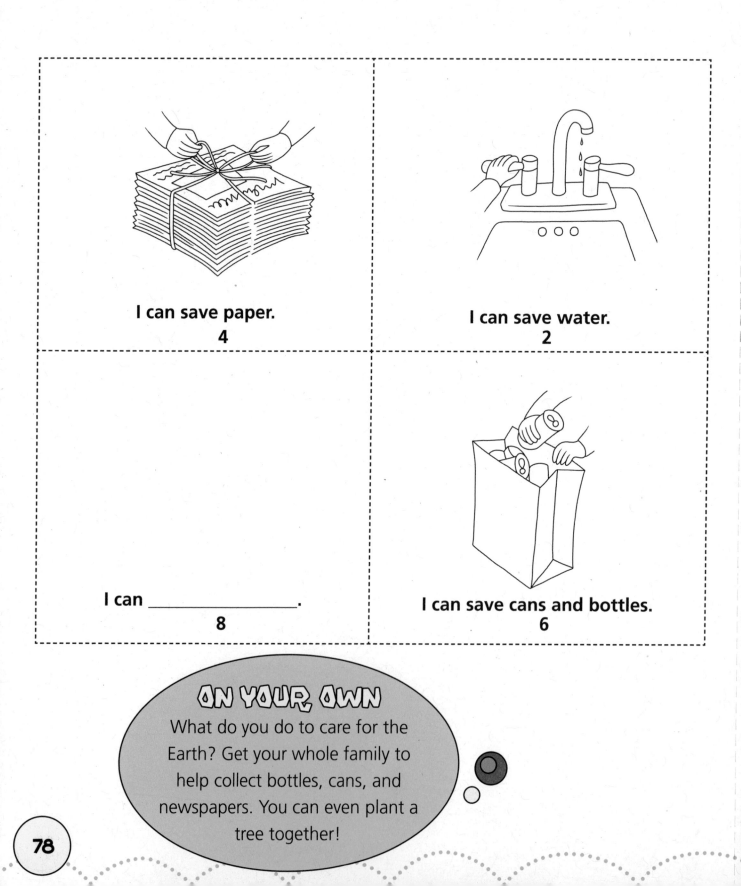

I can save paper.
4

I can save water.
2

I can _____.
8

I can save cans and bottles.
6

ON YOUR OWN

What do you do to care for the Earth? Get your whole family to help collect bottles, cans, and newspapers. You can even plant a tree together!

TIME MATCH

Draw a line matching the times on the clocks.

(clock ~11:00)	`4:00`
(clock ~6:00)	`11:00`
(clock ~6:30)	`8:00`
(clock ~12:30)	`3:30`
(clock ~8:00)	`12:30`
(clock ~3:30)	`6:30`

ON YOUR OWN

Play a time game! Write the numbers 1 to 12 on separate pieces of paper. Place them in a circle on the floor, like a giant clock face. Have a parent ask you to show different times by hopping from number to number. For example, to show 3:00, you would hop to 3 for the hour hand and 12 for the minute hand.

CAN YOU COUNT?

Count the objects in each row.
Then draw more objects to make a total of **15**.
On the line, write how many objects you added.

1.	7
2.	
3.	
4.	
5.	
6.	
7.	
8.	

ON YOUR OWN

Get a set of dominoes. Count the dots on each domino. Then put two dominoes together. Count all the dots. Mix up all the dominoes. Choose many pairs to count.

JUGGLING COLORS

Trace the words in the picture.
Then color this picture using the color words.

orange

purple

pink

black

red

blue

blue

yellow

blue

brown

brown

black

pink

pink

pink

blue

blue

green

green

green

green

SEEING SOUNDS

Say the name for each picture. Listen to the first sounds you hear.
Write the beginning sounds for each picture. Then write the words in the
crossword puzzle.

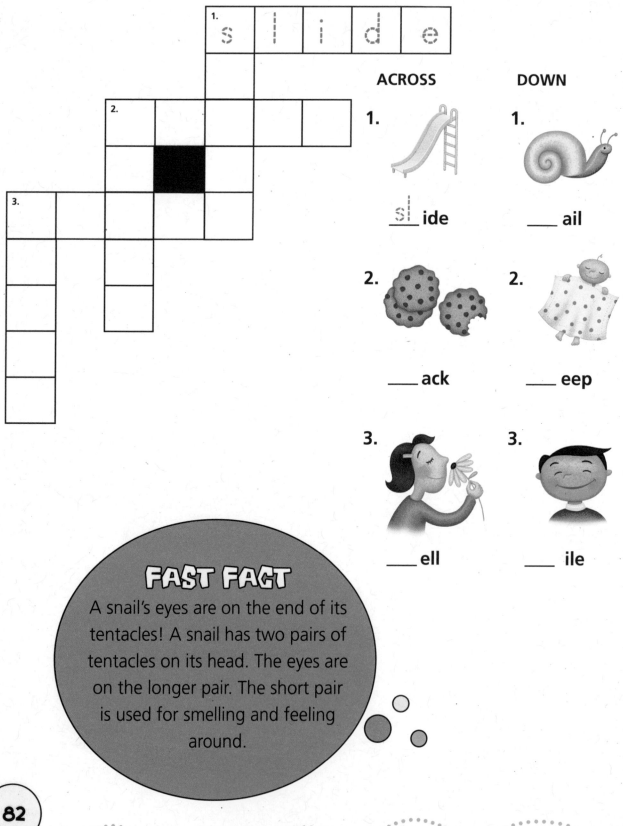

ACROSS

1.
sl ide

2.
___ ack

3.
___ ell

DOWN

1.
___ ail

2.
___ eep

3.
___ ile

FAST FACT

A snail's eyes are on the end of its
tentacles! A snail has two pairs of
tentacles on its head. The eyes are
on the longer pair. The short pair
is used for smelling and feeling
around.

HEALTHY HABITS

Unscramble the word for each sentence. Write it on the line.

1. Before dinner, I S A W H my hands.

W __ash_____

2. I eat good O D F O to stay healthy and strong.

F _____

3. I H R S B U my teeth twice a day.

B _____

4. I wear a E H T E M L when I ride my bike.

H _____

5. I drink L I K M for strong bones.

M _____

6. I cross the T S T E R E with an adult.

S _____

ON YOUR OWN

Exercising is fun! Exercise every day to stay healthy. You can do sit-ups and jumping jacks, ride a bike, take a walk, go swimming, jump rope, play hopscotch, and play outdoor games like softball. Keep track of what you do each week.

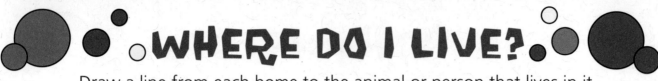

WHERE DO I LIVE?

Draw a line from each home to the animal or person that lives in it.

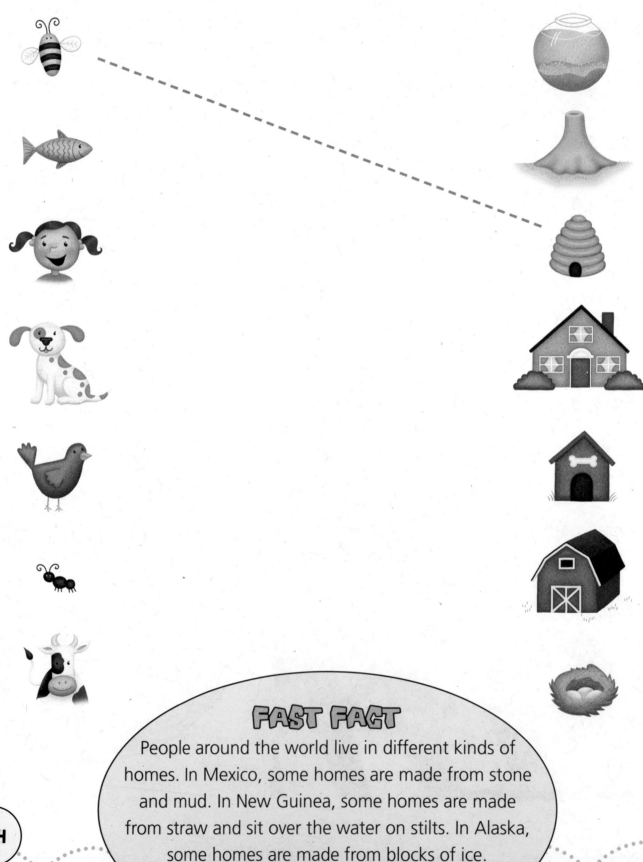

FAST FACT

People around the world live in different kinds of homes. In Mexico, some homes are made from stone and mud. In New Guinea, some homes are made from straw and sit over the water on stilts. In Alaska, some homes are made from blocks of ice.

Look at the graph. Then answer the questions.

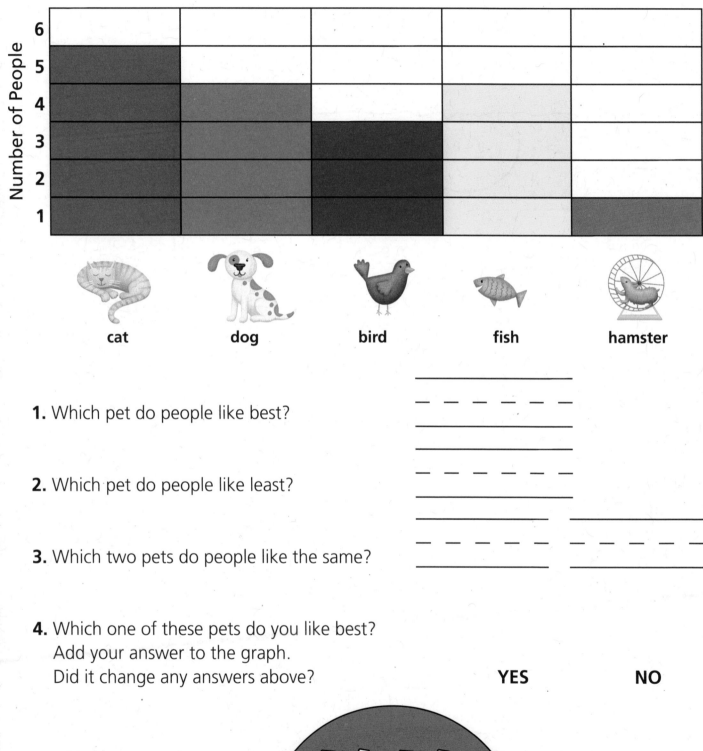

Number of People

cat   dog   bird   fish   hamster

1. Which pet do people like best?

_____

2. Which pet do people like least?

_____

3. Which two pets do people like the same?

_____

4. Which one of these pets do you like best?
Add your answer to the graph.
Did it change any answers above?   **YES   NO**

FAST FACT
Some people own unusual
pets, such as crickets,
pot-bellied pigs, skunks,
and hissing cockroaches!

85

DESERT LIFE

Color **red** in the areas that equal the numbers **0** or **1**.
Color **green** in the areas that equal the numbers **2** or **3**.
Color **blue** in the areas that equal **4** or **5**.
Color **brown** in the areas that equal **6** or **7**.
Color **yellow** in the areas that equal **8** or **9**.

9 – 0

4 – 0

9 – 4

9 – 3

6 – 0

8 – 1

7 – 0

8 – 2

7 – 0

9 – 2

10 – 4

4 – 2

5 – 4

11 – 3

10 – 2

5 – 2

0 – 0

2 – 0

3 – 3

3 – 2

11 – 2

FAST FACT

The world's largest desert is the
Sahara Desert. It is located in Africa.
At more than 3.5 million square
miles, it is almost as big as the
whole United States!

FAT CATS

Write a color word from the box to finish each rhyme. The word should rhyme with the last word in the first line. Color the cat the matching color!

green	pink	brown	black
blue	yellow	white	red

1. Fuzzy is a happy fellow,
 I think I will color him __yellow__!

3. Sheba's tail is long and lean,
 I think I will color her _____!

5. Chester roams around the town,
 I think I will color him _____!

7. Tomcat sleeps upon my bed,
 I think I will color him _____!

2. Snowy's fur is clean and bright,
 I think I will color her _____!

4. Tiny curls up in the sink,
 I think I will color him _____!

6. Misty loves to purr and mew,
 I think I will color her _____!

8. Silky laps milk for a snack,
 I think I will color her _____!

ON THE FARM

Unscramble the name of each farm animal. Write it on the line.

1.		W C O	COW
2.		E H N	
3.		E P E H S	
4.		O G D	
5.		G I P	
6.		U K D C	
7.		T C A	
8.		T A G O	

FAST FACT

Pigs do not sweat. To stay cool, they roll in mud. When the mud dries, the pigs scratch the mud off on a tree or fence. This leaves them nice and clean!

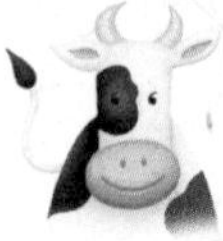

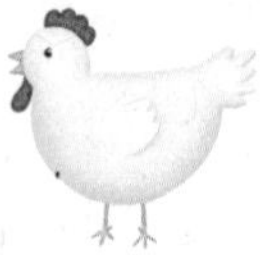

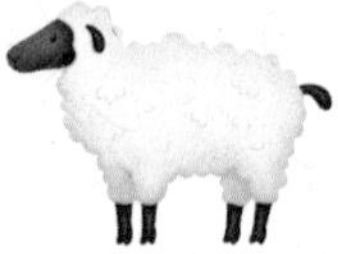

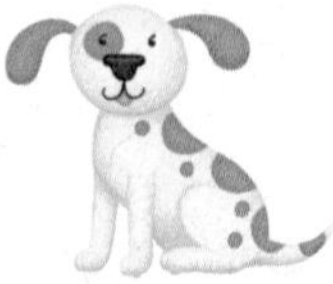

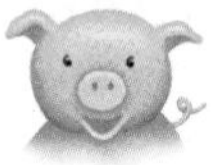

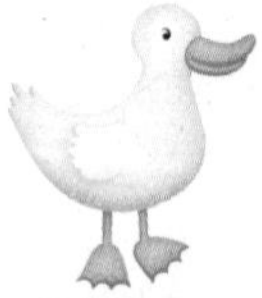

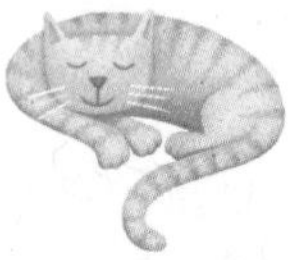

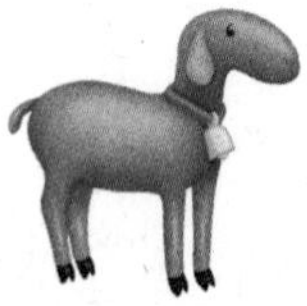

SECRET MESSAGE

Use the letter code below to write a secret message.
Write the letters that go with the shapes in the boxes.

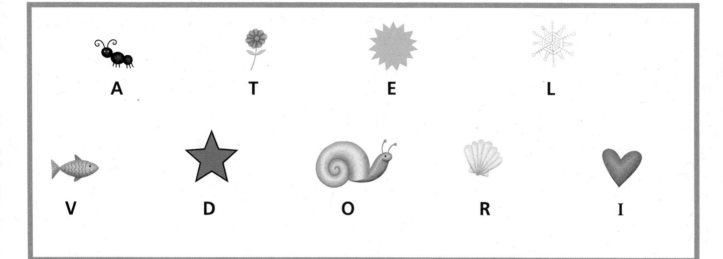

ON YOUR OWN
Use the shapes to write other secret messages. Give them to a family member or friend to solve!

MIRROR MAGIC

Do you know what these shapes will look like in a mirror?
Find out by drawing each shape on the edge of an index card and
pressing it up against a mirror. What do you see? Draw the pictures
you see in the mirror below.

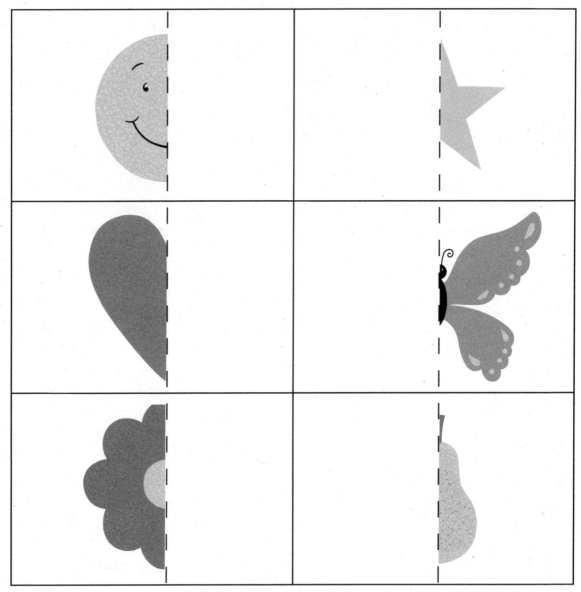

ON YOUR OWN

Make some mirror magic! Place a small
mirror in a clear glass of water. Place it on a
sunny windowsill. Make sure the sun shines
on the mirror and light is reflected on a wall.
What do you see? What happens when you
move the mirror?

LET'S TRAVEL!

Look at each picture. How does it travel?
Draw a line from the picture to the word **air**, **water**, or **land**.

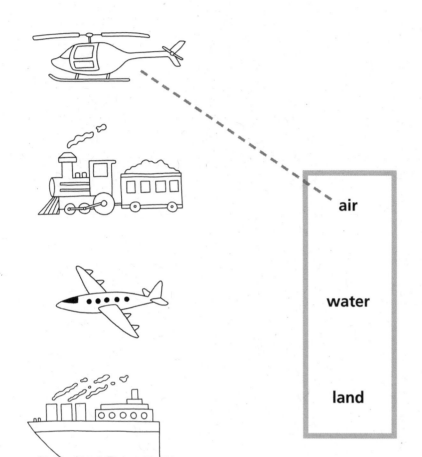

air

water

land

ON YOUR OWN

What is your favorite way to travel? Have you been on a train or plane? Do you ride a bike? Have you ever been on a big boat? Write words or sentences about one way you like to travel. Then draw a picture to go with what you wrote.

SUMMER READING LIST

Here are some books for readers going into first grade
to enjoy during the summer months.

From the Bellybutton of the Moon and Other Summer Poems written by Francisco X. Alarcón illustrated by Maya Christina Gonzales
This collection of 22 English and Spanish poems celebrates the simple joys of summertime in Mexico. Vivid, colorful paintings make the poems come alive.

My Visit to the Aquarium by Aliki
Journey underwater at the aquarium to discover the incredible world of fish, crustaceans, and mollusks. Beautiful watercolor illustrations create a sense of water and movement.

Castles, Caves, and Honeycombs
written by Linda Ashman
illustrated by Lauren Stringer
This book explores all of the snug, comfortable places animals call home.

The Velveteen Rabbit
written by Margery Williams Bianco
illustrated by William Nicholson
This classic story tells of an old, tattered toy rabbit who is loved so much that he becomes real.

The Little House by Virginia L. Burton
Explore the world of long ago and today by watching one little house through the years. At first, it stands alone in the country but, finally, ends up surrounded by apartment buildings in the big city.

Fish Eyes: A Book You Can Count On
by Lois Ehlert
Explore numbers, shapes, colors, and more by following a little fish who keeps the counting going, from page to page.

Out of the Ocean by Debra Frasier
Perfect for summer, this book explores all the wonderful things you can find on the seashore. A glossary provides more information on shells, plants, and even messages in bottles.

Jump, Frog, Jump! written by Robert Kalan illustrated by Byron Barton
In this classic children's tale, a frog leaps from danger over and over again. Repetitive text draws you into the suspense of what might happen next!

Pigs Aplenty, Pigs Galore! by David McPhail
This silly rhyming book follows a herd of partying pigs as they take over the narrator's house. Watch as they make oatmeal in the sink, play music, order pizzas, and more.

Amelia Bedelia written by Peggy Parish illustrated by Fritz Siebel
Follow the adventures of this very "literal" housekeeper as she "dusts" the furniture by putting dust on it and "draws the drapes" by drawing a picture of them.

Too Many Tamales written by Gary Soto illustrated by Ed Martinez
Maria feels so grown up wearing her mother's apron and helping to make tamales. When she puts on her mother's diamond ring, it disappears into the tamales! How will she ever find it?

Somewhere Today: A Book of Peace
written by Shelley Moore Thomas
photographs by Eric Futran
Peace begins with simple words and gestures, as affirmed in the gentle prose in this text. Photographs show children being kind and helpful to each other all around the world.

The Seashore Book written by Charlotte Zolotow illustrated by Wendell Minor
A mother describes the seashore to her son, who has never been there. The poem is bursting with the vibrant colors, sounds, and sights of the seashore.

SUMMER ACTIVITIES AND PROJECTS

Become a Better Reader

This summer try to look at and read books whenever you can! While you read:

- Look at the cover and read the title. Guess what the book might be about.
- Practice turning the pages from right to left.
- Try to guess what might happen next in the story.
- Read aloud with a parent. Take turns reading different characters.
- Run your finger under the words as you read. Look at how words go from left to right across the page.
- When you are done with a story, retell it to a parent.
- Make up or write a new ending to the story.

Day and Night

Take special walks with a parent. First, take a walk in the morning. Describe what you see, hear, and smell. Then, take a walk in the evening. Describe what you see, hear, and smell. How was your morning walk different from your night walk?

Dig and Describe

Have a parent bury small objects, such as shells, rocks, and plastic dinosaurs in a bucket or box of sand. Then dig up each item. Describe the item's color, shape, size, and texture.

A Guessing Game

Each week have a parent fill a jar with small objects, such as jellybeans or pennies. Guess how many items are in the jar. Fill the jar with different objects each week.

Lovely Letters

Practice writing letters and words. Try it with pencil on a sheet of paper. You can also practice writing on the sidewalk using chalk or a jar of water and a paintbrush.

Match It!

Play a matching game with index cards. Match addition and subtraction facts, rhyming words, short-vowel and long-vowel words, number words and numerals, color words and colors, and more!

Mix Your Own Colors

Use finger paint to mix different colors together. Make new colors. Give your new colors fun names!

Nature Hike

With a parent, go on a nature hike! Look at the shapes, colors, and sizes of bugs, leaves, flowers, plants, and animals you see and hear on your hike.

Pretty Patterns

Collect buttons in all shapes and colors. Use the buttons to make patterns. Begin simple patterns for a parent to finish.

ANSWER KEY

Page 6

Page 7
2. 5
3. 5
4. 4
5. 7
6. 6
7. 4
8. 8

Page 8
The objects with these numbers are circled:
2. 10
3. 6
4. 8
5. 5
6. 9

Page 9
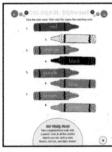

Page 10

Page 11
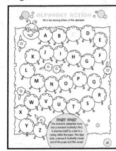

Page 12
2. c
3. b
4. w
5. s
6. h
7. l
8. p
9. g
10. k
11. r
12. d

Page 13
Answers will vary.

Page 14
These combinations are colored the same color:
1/one
2/two
3/three
4/four
5/five
6/six
7/seven
8/eight
9/nine
10/ten

Page 15
2. tennis racket
3. book
4. car
5. tiger
6. elephant

Page 16
2. 11:30
3. 5:30
4. 9:00
5. 12:00
6. 8:30

Page 17

Page 18
2. bear
3. cat
4. deer
5. fox
6. hippo
7. lion
8. mouse
9. owl
10. pig
11. snake
12. whale

Page 19
2. pail
3. dog
4. stop
5. fan
6. jar
7. bed
8. lock

Page 20

Page 21
These pictures are colored:
Girl sharing crayons
Girl helping her friend after bike fall
Boy and girl washing dishes

Page 22
2. square
3. triangle
4. triangle
5. circle
6. square
7. circle
8. square

Page 23
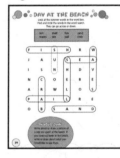

Page 24
2. 4
3. 5
4. 7
5. 5
6. 2
7. 2
8. 6

Page 25
These objects should be colored:
grapes, ape, plane, snake, sail, gate

Page 26
These objects should be colored:
seal, bee, sheep, peas, tree, leaf

Page 27

Page 28
2. forest
3. rain forest
4. ocean

Page 29
This page is complete when the words are traced. Answers to the question will vary.

Page 30
2. 2 quarters
3. 3 dimes, 2 nickels
4. 2 dimes, 1 nickel, 2 pennies; or 3 nickels, 1 dime, 2 pennies

5. 1 quarter, 2 nickels, 3 pennies
6. 2 quarters, 1 dime, 1 penny

Page 31
2. horse
3. chair
4. sneaker
5. crayon
6. flower
7. bike
8. bee

Page 32
2. 3 inches
3. 4 inches
4. 3 inches
5. 5 inches
6. 2 inches

Page 33
Words with 2 letters: in, an, it, at
Words with 3 letters: tan, ran, tin, rat, tar, art, ant
Words with 4 letters: rain
The BIG word: train

Page 34

Page 35
These objects should be colored:
eye, bike, dime, pie, mice, five

Page 36
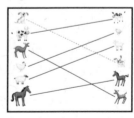

1. puppy
2. chick
3. calf
4. lamb
5. fawn
6. foal

Page 37

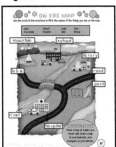

Page 38
2. less
3. more
4. more
5. less
6. less

Page 39
This page is complete when the words are traced and a picture is drawn at the bottom. Answers to the question will vary.

Page 40
2. 7
3. 12
4. 8
5. 2

Page 41

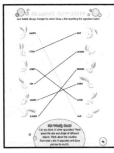

Page 42
2. read
3. boat
4. seal
5. goat
6. bean
7. toad
8. meat

Page 43
These objects should be colored: soap, rope, hoe, toe, bow

Page 44
2. fall
3. summer
4. spring
5. winter
6. fall
7. spring
8. winter
9. fall
10. summer

Page 45

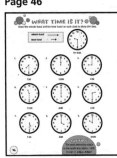

Page 46

Page 47

Page 48

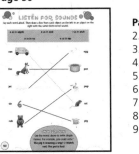

Page 49
These objects are colored: mule, unicorn, spoon, broom, cube, flute, glue

Page 50

Page 51
2. lake, steak
3. bee, sea
4. sock, rock
5. ring, swing
6. rain, plane

Page 52
2. smell
3. hear
4. see
5. taste
6. smell
7. feel
8. see
9. hear

Page 53
2. read
3. fires
4. pet
5. teeth
6. safe

Page 54
2. 1
3. 6
4. 0
5. 1
6. 2
7. 3
8. 2
9. 5

Page 55

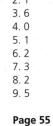

Page 56

Page 57
2. e
3. u
4. e
5. i
6. o
7. a
8. u
9. o

Page 58

Page 59
2. S
3. Q
4. S
5. Q
6. Q
7. S
8. S
9. Q
10. S

Page 60

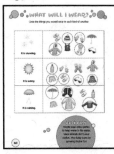

Page 61
These pictures should be colored:
boy on bike, girl in pool, boy playing baseball, boy in canoe, boy at crosswalk, girl putting on sunscreen, girl putting on bandage
These pictures should be crossed out:
girl opening poison bottle, girl rollerblading without helmet, boy in tree, girl jumping on bed, boy at stove

Page 62

Page 63
2. $1 + 7 = 8$
3. $3 + 3 = 6$
4. $4 + 3 = 7$
5. $5 + 3 = 8$
6. $7 + 5 = 12$
7. $2 + 5 = 7$
8. $5 + 5 = 10$

Page 64
2. 2 3 4 5 6 7 8 9
3. 3 3 5 5 7 7 9 9
4. 2 4 6 8 10 12 14 16
5. 10 9 8 7 6 5 4 3

Page 65
Answers will vary.

Page 66
Foods: bread, grapes, beans, milk, pizza
Colors: blue, brown, red, green, yellow
Shapes: circle, triangle, star, square, oval

Page 67
2. girl
3. bird
4. boy
5. dog
6. blue

Page 68
This page is complete when the animals are colored and the words are traced.

Page 69
1. These objects are colored blue: covered wagon, horse and buggy
These objects are colored yellow: car, plane, ship
2. These objects are colored blue: Pony Express, old-fashioned phone, feather pen and inkwell
These objects are colored yellow: computer, cell phone
3. These objects are colored blue: hurricane lamp, washboard
These objects are colored yellow: lightbulb, fridge, microwave oven

Page 70
2. 6¢
3. 12¢
4. 40¢
5. 25¢
6. 36¢
7. 32¢
8. 45¢
9. 42¢
10. 39¢

Page 71
2. 2
3. 3
4. 2
5. 5

6. 1
7. 4
8. 0
9. 6

Page 72
2. night
3. morning
4. morning
5. night
6. morning

Page 73
1. Take out bread, peanut butter, and knife.
2. Take out two pieces of bread.
3. Open peanut butter jar.
4. Spread peanut butter on bread.
5. Put pieces of bread together.
6. Eat! Yum!

Page 74
My family went to the <u>zoo</u>. We had so much fun! First, my <u>dad</u> got me a toy <u>lion</u> at the gift shop. We fed a big gray <u>elephant</u>. We fed him lots of <u>peanuts</u>. Then I saw a funny <u>monkey</u> in a tree! We saw more animals too. The sign told us where to find <u>zebras</u> and <u>snakes</u>. I liked the elephant the best. I love the zoo!

Page 75
1. Fox is the character in the story.
2. The story takes place in a field.
3. Fox was walking in the field.
4. Fox walked away from the grapes.
5. He was thirsty, and he couldn't reach the grapes.

Page 76
Answers will vary.

Pages 77 and 78
The pages are complete when the pages are colored. Children's pictures and ideas for helping the Earth will vary.

Page 79
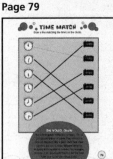

Page 80
2. 5
3. 8
4. 11
5. 8
6. 4
7. 10
8. 6

Page 81
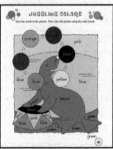

Page 82

Page 83
2. food
3. brush
4. helmet
5. milk
6. street

Page 84
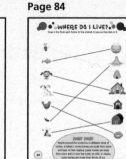

Page 85
1. cat
2. hamster
3. dog and fish
4. Answers will vary.

Page 86

Page 87
2. white
3. green
4. pink
5. brown
6. blue
7. red
8. black

Page 88
2. hen
3. sheep
4. dog
5. pig
6. duck
7. cat
8. goat

Page 89
I love to read!

Page 90

Page 91